GW00750950

THE STORY OF A WEDDING PRESENT ALBUM

VALENTINA

THE STORY OF A WEDDING PRESENT ALBUM

by David Lewis Gedge

with contributions from

Graeme Ramsay
Charles Layton
Pepe le Moko
Terry de Castro
Andrew Scheps

The Friday Project
An imprint of HarperCollins Publishers,
77–85 Fulham Palace Road,
Hammersmith, London W6 8JB,
www.harpercollins.co.uk

First published in Great Britain
in 2012 by The Friday Project
in association with Scopitones.

1

A catalogue record for this book
is available from the British Library.

ISBN 978-0-00-749413-2

Photography by Jessica McMillan
and Andrew Lurcuck.

Typeset by Egelnick and Webb.

Printed and bound in Hong Kong by
Printing Express.

Special thanks to Scott Pack and
Maria Forte.

The Wedding Present would like to dedicate this book to Brian & Marjorie Gedge, Barbara & Donald Ramsay, Nick & Sharon Layton and Andy Bass.

DOWNLOAD INFORMATION

Purchasing this book enables you to access a 'password protected' area within the web site of Scopitones, the home of Cinerama and The Wedding Present.

Inside this protected area you will be able to download the entire *Valentina* long-player for free, together with four extra tracks that were recorded at the same time but not included on the album. You will also be able to download an exclusive video documentary containing footage filmed at the studio and interviews with David Gedge and the other band members.

You can find the protected area at...

http://www.scopitones.co.uk/protected-area

...where you will also find instructions on how to find the password within the text of this book.

VALENTINA

The renowned recording engineer Steve Albini once told me there were only two studios in the whole of Europe that he'd ever consider using. Albini's prone to making outrageous-sounding pronouncements like this, but, though I believe they're sometimes designed to shock, they're usually not without substance. One of the studios he recommended was Black Box near Nantes and the other was Abbey Road in London.
I decided that France would be an interesting location to record the tracks that would ultimately constitute The Wedding Present's eighth studio album, *Valentina*, so I started the ball rolling by emailing David Odlum at Black Box. One of the first things I noticed from David's messages was that his English was immaculate and this eased any fears I might've had of Anglo-French communication problems. My knowledge of French is limited and so I wrote my own messages in the clearest English I could muster and avoided colloquialisms. I think David probably thought my messages were quite oddly written. This is because David is an Irishman.

The late Iain Burgess, an English recording engineer who was noted for his work in Chicago during the 1980s, set up Black Box in the early 1990s with his friend Peter Deimel, who's German. Amongst the bands Burgess recorded in the U.S.A. was Big Black, featuring... Steve Albini. It's claimed that he was hugely influential on Albini himself and so I guess that's from where the recommendation originated.

So, having made up my mind, on 1 August 2011 we loaded up the car with all manner of instruments and accessories and set off down the Channel Tunnel. In retrospect, we'd weighed down my trusty Mercedes for no reason: Black Box is equipped with considerably more guitars [including many built by Peter's brother Frank] and effects pedals than we'd ever have needed, together with a stack of technophile-thrilling amplifiers.

It was a long, hot drive to the picturesque village of Noyant La Gravoyere and so, after getting more than a little lost, it was with some relief that we pulled into the studio grounds. The Black Box complex is housed within a farmhouse in the French countryside and, as we drove up the gravel path, David himself came out to greet us, offer us drinks and show us round the accommodation.

It turns out that David used to be in a band called The Frames who often covered the Weddi Present song 'Octopussy' in their live set and definitely proved to be helpful to be working wi someone who was familiar with Wedding Prese history. David, Peter and Peter's girlfriend, Sylvi were extremely welcoming and their hospitality was matched by their extensive knowledge of recording techniques, although the fact that we were on a farm led to the occasional odd conversation. One minute we'd be discussing the virtues of the studio mixing-desk [a Flicking N24 from the 1960s, for those who are intereste and then Peter would break off to ask David if t chickens had been fed.

All bands make records differently. Some peo will install themselves into a studio, 'jam' fo three weeks and then fiddle with it for six mo Others will painstakingly construct recordings la by layer, one instrument at a time. Some recc everything as if they were playing a live concer like The Beatles used to do! The technique f the making of *Valentina* ended up being kind a combination of all three.

Once the equipment had been set up and covered with microphones, we played through t songs live and everything... drums, bass, guita even my rough vocals... was recorded onto 2 tape. But in the back of our minds we knew th only the drums had to be perfect at this point This was because our drummer, Charles Layto would be leaving France for another engagem in just two days. But as long as all of Charlie parts were up to scratch, we could replace t bass and guitar parts later by over-dubbing th onto the multi-track.

LOVE
BLACK
La Dionnaie

For the recordings I stood in the 'control room' with David and Peter so that I could speak to them without having to rely on 'talkback' through microphones and headphones. It's also useful to hear the sounds being recorded as they come out of the studio speakers, because the microphone can alter the way an instrument sounds and sometimes the engineer will manipulate the signal through the mixing desk, anyway. Our bass player, Pepe le Moko, stood in the 'drum room' next to Charlie. I think it's beneficial for the bass player to be next to the drummer so that they can lock into the rhythm. Guitarist Graeme Ramsay found himself somewhere in-between the control-room and the drum-room, surrounded by a forest of amplifiers and keyboards. Black Box is made up of quite a lengthy series of old barns, so we were all actually standing about 30 metres from each other.

At the end of each performance, the rest of the band would march through to join me in the control room to listen to the recording and decide if the take was a 'keeper.' This isn't as easy as it sounds. Ultimately, not only did we need the drums to be good but also the song had to have the right 'feel'. The drums may be faultless, but if the performance feels stiff, the fact that's in perfect time is cold comfort. It's tricky because you have to balance the temptation for doing songs over and over with losing the character of the performance. Also people... and the drummer, specifically... become tired as the day progresses. So it can be quite stressful, but it's also exciting. Being in the studio is exhilarating really... it's one of the best parts of our job. But there can be a lot of waiting around, too. Even with Charlie only being there for two days, he still played a fair deal of table tennis while the engineers were setting up the next track.

The early part of the recording went well and this was due, in no small part, to Charlie. Recording the drums for seventeen songs in two days is no mean feat but he buckled down and completed the task with aplomb. This gave us plenty of time to fix guitar and bass parts under the watchful gaze of David, Peter and Titi, the studio dog. Titi wasn't actually allowed in the studio, so she sat, woefully, by the open door, peering in at us.

After Charlie took off, Graeme, Pepe and I finished off our parts properly, although much of what Pepe had played didn't need to be replaced; she's such a professional! But then, with the bass... how hard can it be? Ha, ha. She just dropped in to repair the odd note, only playing the whole part over if we decided that the track needed a different bass sound or tuning. Graeme and I took much longer. We used the time that Charlie had bought us to experiment with the daunting array of guitars, amplifiers and effects pedals, auditioning them against each other as well as the bass and drum parts that had been recorded, before deciding on the right sound for each song. I think Graeme was apprehensive about recording guitar because he feels more confident on the drums, his first instrument. (He was actually the drummer on the previous Wedding Present album, *El Rey*). But he needn't have been, he recorded some very intricate guitar parts with panache and then went on to round off our recording time at Black Box by adding some piano and even a piece recorded on an ancient harmonium that we found outside in the courtyard. At the end of the final day's recording we trundled triumphantly back to the house next to the studio where, each night, we'd eat and sleep. When we switched on the television, the first thing we saw was Graeme, playing the drums live in 2008 in front of thousands of people at 'Les Vieilles Charrues,' France's biggest music festival, which was filmed for French TV.

Once we had all the backing tracks recorded, the album was starting to take shape, but it was still a long way from what you'd call finished. We were only supposed to be in France for six days but we decided to add another day so that David and Peter were able to provide us with a rough mix of the album to take away. They toiled well into the night of this extra day in order to do this!

Following our trip to France, I decided to take advantage of 21st Century technology and an eight-hour difference in time zones to add vocals simultaneously to the backing tracks in both Los Angeles, California and Brighton, England. You only really need a small studio to record singing, since it's essentially just you and a decent microphone in a booth. I recorded my parts at The Laundry Room, a first-rate space owned by our friend, the interestingly named Ulysses Noriega, in L.A. and then each night would send files over to Brighton so that Pepe could add her bits while we slept. Samuel Beer-Pearce, who has occasionally 'stood in' on both guitar and drums for The Wedding Present live, recorded Pepe's singing in his home studio by the sea. Meanwhile, our former bass player, Terry de Castro, popped into Uly's to add some of her dulcet tones to the pot, while Japanese songstress Sayaka Amano emailed me a vocal contribution from Tokyo.

With the recording completed, it was time for Graeme, my main co-writer on Valentina, to fly over to join me in California, where we mixed the album at Andrew Scheps' studio in Van Nuys. Our occasional live sound engineer, Pete Magdaleno, had introduced Andrew to us and, to be honest I had initially been a little nervous about his track record. Andrew is a multiple Grammy award winning producer and mixer who has worked with artists as distinguished and diverse as Adele, Iggy Pop, Metallica and Johnny Cash. But I needn't have worried... Andrew is very down-to-earth and instantly likeable and, most importantly, gave us everything we wanted in the mix and more besides, by preserving the 'band in a room' realness of the recording, while still delivering generous punch, clarity and power. It takes great ears and an extensive knowledge to fit in so much without compromising the 'true' feel and sound of the instruments. We'd actually already benefited from Andrew's talents as early as the previous summer, when he'd attended one of our rehearsals in Brighton and thrown in just enough good arrangement ideas for us to know that he could improve the songs without altering them too much. After that rehearsal, we went for lunch, but when the bill came, I realised I'd left my wallet at the studio and had to ask Andrew for some money. 'Ah... I see how this works!' he said.

After a week or so of intensive mixing in Andrew's studio, we chose the songs for the album and then Graeme picked the order in which they'd go on. You might think that we'd simply choose our ten favourite tracks. Not so. An album has to have a beginning and an end and flow seamlessly from one point to the next, incorporating light and shade and changes of texture and pace. Often good songs have to be left off the finished LP because there's simply no place for them.

Finally, Andrew sent the files over to London to be mastered by Andy Pearce and Matt Wortham. Mastering engineers run a final, more 'technical' ear over the recordings and can make suggestions about level and tone before assembling the finished master. But, with regard to *Valentina*, Andy felt that such a good job had already been done that he had nothing to fix. Meanwhile, the designers Egelnick And Webb were already busy poring over some curious photographs taken by Jessica McMillan for the sleeve as they listened to the mixes of the songs. At this point, you start to feel that an album is out of your hands. You never feel that it's completely finished of course... you would always go back and replace a line or switch the song order or something... if you could. But at a certain point you have to tell yourself that you've done enough. It sounds right, it looks right... and it feels right. It's time to let everyone else see what you've been up to for the last three years...

David Lewis Gedge,
Brighton, England, 2012

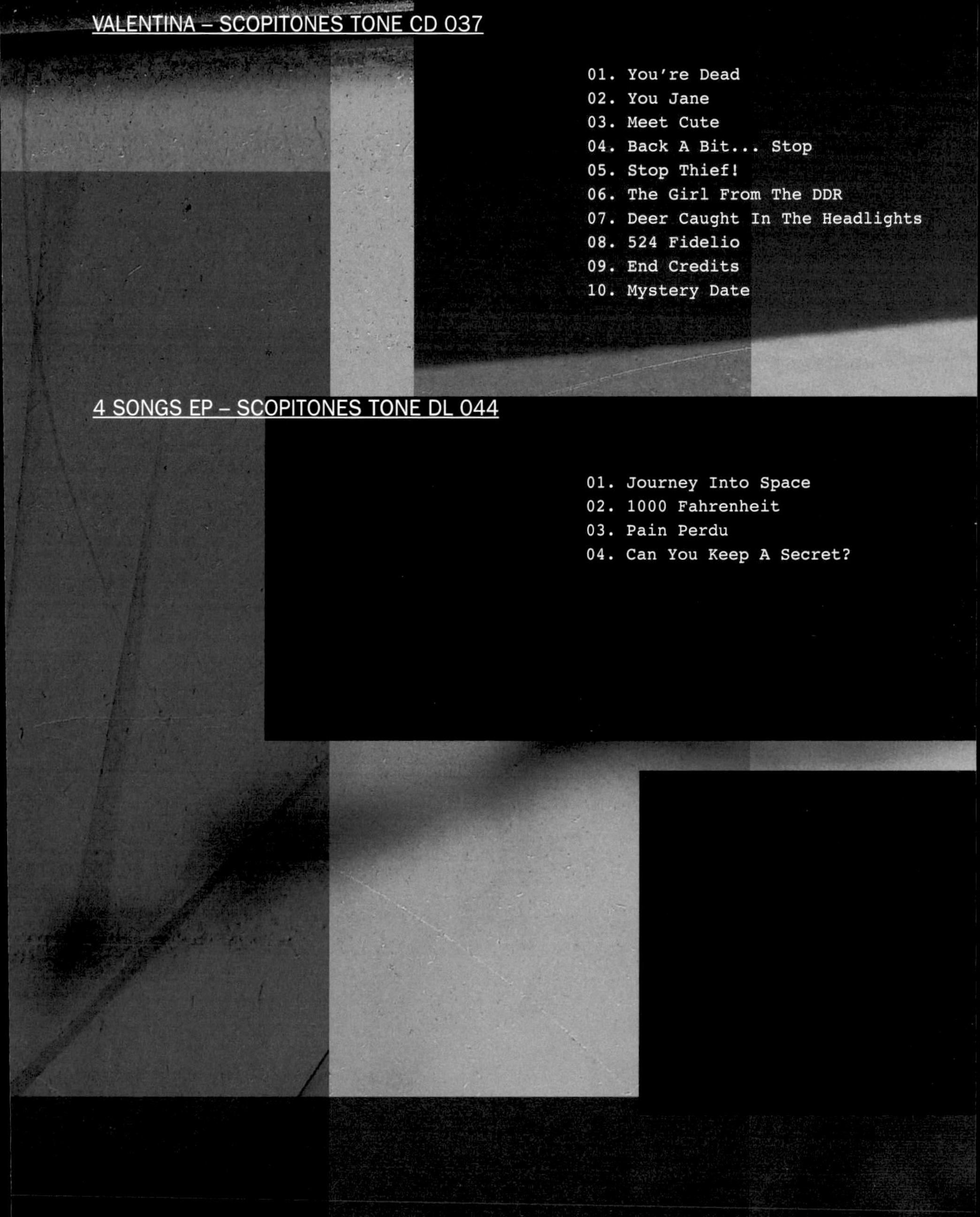

VALENTINA – SCOPITONES TONE CD 037

01. You're Dead
02. You Jane
03. Meet Cute
04. Back A Bit... Stop
05. Stop Thief!
06. The Girl From The DDR
07. Deer Caught In The Headlights
08. 524 Fidelio
09. End Credits
10. Mystery Date

4 SONGS EP – SCOPITONES TONE DL 044

01. Journey Into Space
02. 1000 Fahrenheit
03. Pain Perdu
04. Can You Keep A Secret?

01. YOU'RE DEAD

WHEN YOU BURIED YOUR FACE INTO MY CHEST
(YOUR LITTLE HIDING PLACE)
I WOULD NEVER HAVE GUESSED WHAT A LITTLE CHEAT YOU A
WHAT A LIAR YOU TURNED OUT TO BE
HOW WE EVEN GOT THIS FAR IS A MYSTERY

I KNOW YOU'RE NOT DISTRAUGHT, SO YOU CAN LOSE THE FRC
YOU MUST KNOW YOU JUST CAUGHT ME
WHEN MY GUARD WAS DOWN
AND WHEN YOU ASKED ME: "ARE WE BREAKING-UP?"
YOU KNEW, ALREADY, WHAT THE ANSWER WAS
AND, NO, WE WON'T BE MAKING UP BECAUSE...

BANG! BANG! YOU'RE DEAD!
THIS IS OUT OF CONTROL AND I AM SICK OF THE WHOLE
SHEBANG, I SAID
AM I MAKING IT CLEAR? I WANT YOU OUT OF HERE!

I USED TO THINK THAT I'D RATHER FIGHT WITH YOU
THAN FALL IN LOVE WITH SOMEBODY NEW
I THINK I NEEDED SHAKING UP;
I'M NOT GOING BACK TO HOW IT WAS
THIS TIME WE'RE NOT MAKING UP BECAUSE...

BANG! BANG! YOU'RE DEAD!
THIS IS OUT OF CONTROL AND I AM SICK OF THE WHOLE
SHEBANG, I SAID
AM I MAKING IT CLEAR? I WANT YOU OUT OF HERE!

POW! POW! YOU'RE DEAD!
THIS IS OUT OF CONTROL AND I AM SICK OF THE WHOLE,
BIG ROW, I SAID
AM I MAKING IT CLEAR? I WANT YOU OUT OF HERE!

SO NOW YOU WANT TO APOLOGISE
WELL, THAT COMES AS NO SURPRISE
BECAUSE I CAN READ YOU AND I DON'T NEED YOU
THIS TIME YOU WENT TOO FAR AND I KNOW EXACTLY
WHAT YOU ARE
I UNDERSTAND YOU AND I CAN'T STAND YOU
BUT HOW COME, DURING TIMES LIKE THIS,
I STILL WANT YOUR TOUCH AND I WANT YOUR KISS
IT'S INSANE AND I CAN'T EXPLAIN WHY
YOU'RE NOT THE ONE FOR ME ALTHOUGH I JUST CAN'T SE
TO LET YOU GO
YOU APPAL ME
OKAY CALL ME

'This was one of the first of the 'new' songs to be written. I remember Graeme had the riff and a suggestion for a tom tom beat for the drums. I played around with various ideas and finally settled on something during the 2010 *Bizarro* tour. It's a lot of fun to play, though I would probably say that about any songs I play drums on!'
Charles Layton

'It's kind of a bleak title... but it's meant to convey the feeling that it would be convenient if you could just eliminate someone who's annoying you... like you can in a video game. And then resurrect them when you want them back!'
David Gedge

'I remember when I was mixing this, all of a sudden the instrumental sections went into their own sonic space. I had to force myself to back away from the console before I screwed it up. David's reading of 'OK, call me...' still makes me laugh.'
Andrew Scheps

'The extended end section came about when we chose this tune to be the last song in the set before we launched into playing *Bizarro* live on the 2010 tour. During the live performance we cycled round the final chord sequence while our live sound engineer played multiple recordings of the legendary BBC presenter John Peel introducing The Wedding Present on the radio. But then, after the tour, when we played the song without Peel's voice we found that the end part still worked well and that the piece had developed into a little 'bass solo' section, which was kind of unusual...'
David Gedge

'The end of 'You're Dead' is one of the rare soft parts on *Valentina*. Whilst I mostly play with a plectrum, I play the little bass plucking bit with fingers... and I chose a warmer sound with more bottom end on the amp, in contrast to the usually slightly more trebly bass sound of the record.'
Pepe le Moko

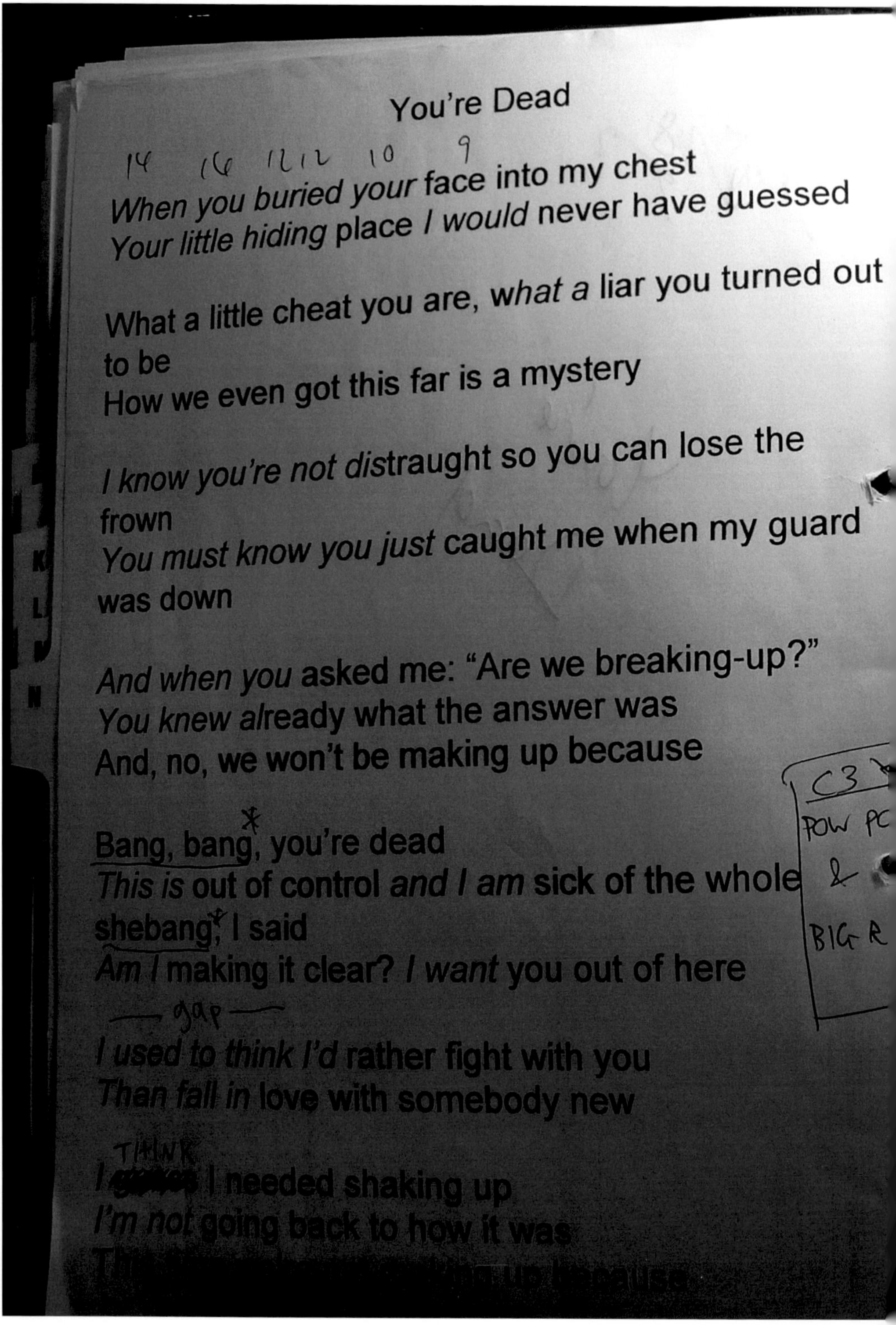

You're Dead

14 16 12 12 10 9

When you buried your face into my chest
Your little hiding place I would never have guessed

What a little cheat you are, what a liar you turned out to be
How we even got this far is a mystery

I know you're not distraught so you can lose the frown
You must know you just caught me when my guard was down

And when you asked me: "Are we breaking-up?"
You knew already what the answer was
And, no, we won't be making up because

Bang, bang, you're dead
This is out of control and I am sick of the whole shebang, I said
Am I making it clear? I want you out of here

— gap —

I used to think I'd rather fight with you
Than fall in love with somebody new

THINK
I ~~guess~~ I needed shaking up
I'm not going back to how it was
Th[illegible] up because

C3
POW PC
&
BIG R

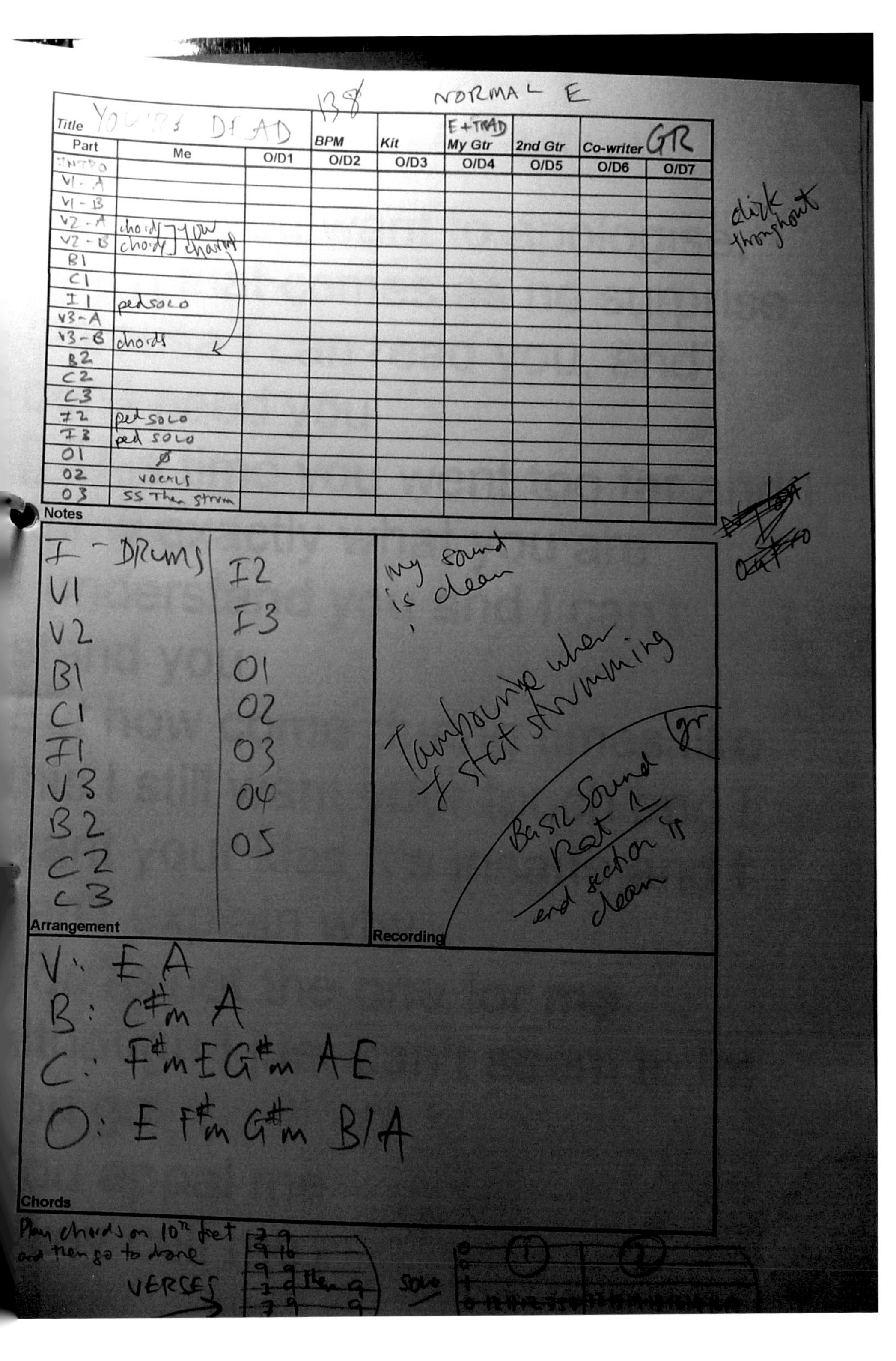

Title YOU'RE DEAD
138
NORMAL E
BPM
Kit
E+TRAD
My Gtr
2nd Gtr
Co-writer GR
Part
Me
O/D1
O/D2
O/D3
O/D4
O/D5
O/D6
O/D7
INTRO
V1-A
V1-B
V2-A chords
V2-B chords
low chords
B1
C1
I1 ped SOLO
V3-A
V3-B chords
B2
C2
C3
I2 ped SOLO
I3 ped SOLO
O1 Ø
O2 VOCALS
O3 SS Then strum
click throughout
Notes
I - DRUMS
V1
V2
B1
C1
I1
V3
B2
C2
C3
I2
I3
O1
O2
O3
O4
O5
Arrangement
my sound is clean
Tambourine when I start strumming
gr
Basic Sound Rat 1
end section is clean
Recording
V: E A
B: C#m A
C: F#m E G#m A E
O: E F#m G#m B/A
Chords
Play chords on 10th fret and then go to drone
VERSES
SOLO

'The opening riff for this song came to me while I was waiting for a lift to football training. It certainly has the feel of going somewhere or being about to go somewhere. I don't think it was altered from that point and I (somewhat optimistically) thought it should be a single before the song was even written.'
Graeme Ramsay

02. YOU JANE

I HOPE YOU FIND WHAT YOU'RE LOOKING FOR
DO YOU EVEN KNOW WHAT THAT IS, ANYMORE?

I HOPE HE'S REALLY THE ONE WHO WILL MAKE
ALL YOUR DREAMS COME TRUE
BUT IF, BY SOME UNEXPECTED CHANCE,
THIS DOESN'T TURN OUT TO BE
YOUR FAIRY TALE ROMANCE

JUST DON'T COME CRYING TO ME
DON'T COME CRYING TO ME
THIS IS THE WAY THAT YOU WANT IT TO BE
SO DON'T COME CRYING

THERE'S REALLY NO NEED TO EXPLAIN,
HE'S TARZAN AND YOU'RE JANE
HE'S BOGART, YOU'RE BACALL AND I'M SURE
HE HAS IT ALL

JUST DON'T COME CRYING TO ME
DON'T COME CRYING TO ME
THIS IS THE WAY THAT YOU WANT IT TO BE
SO DON'T COME CRYING

THERE'S REALLY NO NEED TO EXPLAIN,
HE'S TARZAN AND YOU'RE JANE
HE'S BOGART, YOU'RE BACALL AND I'M SURE
HE HAS IT ALL
HE DOESN'T HAVE TO TRY TOO HARD,
HE'S GABLE, YOU'RE LOMBARD
HE'S RICHARD AND YOU'RE LIZ
I GUESS YOU'RE LUCKY TO BE HIS

'Graeme hadn't heard Pepe's layered backing vocal idea until he arrived in L.A. for the mix and, to be honest, I was dreading playing it for him. I just thought he'd hate it, whereas I liked it a lot... even though it sounds a bit like Yes – the, erm, progressive rock band. On the way to Andrew's studio I popped a CD into the car stereo and crossed my fingers, but he went totally the other way and said that the Yes bit was fine but that he no longer liked the more 'straightforward' chorus backing vocals. Little alterations like that can change the whole course of a song sometimes.'
David Gedge

'As we already had the second drum kit set up in the studio for 'End Credits' - the 'two-drummer' song - we joked that David could double up my snare roll at the very end of this track. I passed him a pair of sticks and said, 'Well go on then!' He often jokes about any instrument that isn't the guitar, 'Well, how hard can it be?' but he did do a good job of it! Trust me... I have seen people that just don't have any rhythm!
Charles Layton

'While I was recording the vocal in Los Angeles, Ulysses, totally unprompted, said: 'Is this the single?' It was entertaining... coming up with the list of Hollywood romances for what I call the 'Cinerama' section; I always enjoy slipping in references like that.'
David Gedge

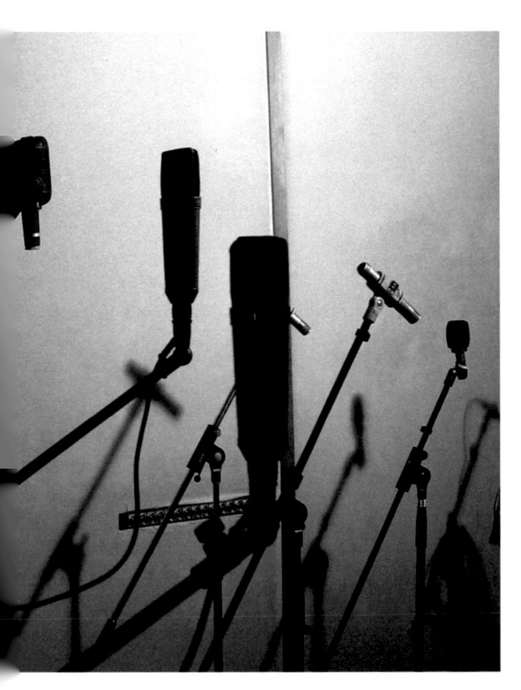

'The demo versions of 'You Jane' only had backing vocals in the choruses. When I listened to the rough mix, however, I felt that there was something lacking in the 'instrumental verse' section, so I tried out a couple of vocal ideas... layering harmonies over them. It's not a common thing for The Wedding Present to do but it worked surprisingly well and that's what you hear on the final version. I think the singing there gave that part an unexpected twist, whereas the original chorus backing vocals were dropped.'
Pepe le Moko

'A 'meet cute' is a plot device used in films. It's a contrived meeting... like in a romantic comedy where the hero and heroine meet by chance after hailing the same taxi or something. I recently found out that Charlie shares my secret affection for romantic comedies!'
David Gedge

3. MEET CUTE

I'D NEVER MET HER BEFORE I FOUND THE HEEL
THAT CAME OFF HER SHOE
I LAUGHED WHEN SHE SWORE
HER LIPS WERE RED AND FULL
I SAID: "I THINK I WANT TO KISS YOU"
SHE SAID: "WHEN WILL YOU KNOW FOR SURE?"

I SAID: "IT'S TOO COLD TO SNOW"
SHE SAID: "JUST WHAT EXACTLY DOES THAT MEAN?"
I SAID: "I DON'T KNOW"
WE ORDERED MORE DRINKS
SHE SAID: "TELL ME WHERE YOU'VE BEEN
AND WHERE YOU WANT TO GO"

AND AM I REALLY SITTING HERE?
THIS IS A STORY WITH INTRIGUE
BECAUSE, IN CASE IT ISN'T CLEAR,
YOU'RE REALLY WAY OUT OF MY LEAGUE

AND THIS IS REALLY JUST TOO GOOD TO BE TRUE
I HAVE TO PINCH MYSELF BECAUSE I'M HERE WITH YOU

AND AM I REALLY SITTING HERE?
THIS IS A STORY WITH INTRIGUE
BECAUSE, IN CASE IT ISN'T CLEAR,
YOU'RE REALLY WAY OUT OF MY LEAGUE

AND AM I REALLY SITTING HERE?
THIS IS A STORY WITH INTRIGUE
BECAUSE, IN CASE IT ISN'T CLEAR,
YOU'RE REALLY WAY OUT OF MY LEAGUE

'I love the big intro and choruses of this song. Loud, crunchy guitar and bass sounds – a moment of fame for my bass overdrive pedal! I think it had just the right impact and supports the big guitar sounds perfectly.'
Pepe le Moko

'Graeme and I are on the same wavelength in terms of what we like in noisy drumming, so the beginning of the song was a pleasure for us to play. He just said 'Smack some cymbals over this drone!' Along with 'Deer Caught In The Headlights,' this is one of my favourite songs to play live. The stomping 'Swollen Pickle' guitar pedal part at the end is awesome, too.'
Charles Layton

'The guitar part in the verse came about after looping a 'Minutemen' drumbeat and playing around over the top of it.'
Graeme Ramsay

'I'd be the first to admit that I'm not the most versatile or talented guitarist in the world, but there are certain elements of my sound, like playing an overdriven Stratocaster guitar tuned primarily to the note of E with a metal bottle-neck (which is all over the introduction and end section of this song) that I'm always eager to unleash!'
David Gedge

04. BACK A BIT... STOP!

EVERY SINGLE THING ABOUT MY SO-CALLED LIFE
WAS BORING UNTIL YOU EXPLODED INTO MY
WORLD
AND I CAN SAY, WITHOUT A DOUBT, THE LIAISON
WE'RE EXPLORING HAS SEEN A WHOLE NEW
SIDE OF ME BEING UNFURLED

OF COURSE I'D LOVE TO FALL HEAD OVER HEELS
FOR YOU BUT THERE'S THE QUESTION OF YOUR
LOVELY FIANCÉ
AND I WON'T BE SWAYED AT ALL BY ANY
ARGUMENTS THAT YOU PUT BECAUSE I'VE TOLD
MYSELF WE CAN'T GO ON THIS WAY

SO GET BACK A BIT, GET BACK A BIT,
GET BACK A BIT
BACK A BIT... NOW STOP

SINCE YOU'VE BEGUN TO SHOW WHAT KIND OF
PERSON YOU ARE I THINK I MIGHT HAVE HAD AN
EPIPHANY
THAT'S WHY I NEED TO GO AND THIS MAY SOUND
A LITTLE BIZARRE, BUT I'M GOING BEFORE YOU
DO THE SAME TO ME

SO GET BACK A BIT, GET BACK A BIT,
GET BACK A BIT
BACK A BIT... NOW STOP

HOW DOES A GIRL LIKE YOU GET TO BE A GIRL
LIKE YOU?

'One of my favourites. I remember that we got the instrumental arrangement pretty quickly. Graeme started playing the main guitar riff in rehearsal and Charlie and I just joined in. The idea for the bass part came to me instantly without needing to fiddle around too much. It just felt natural.'
Pepe le Moko

'A rocking song. This is the 'Drive' or 'Kansas' or 'Sucker' of the album, I think. I played around with various different fills and then decided that there was space to put them all in at the end of the verses! The layered, extra guitar that comes in at 2:05 for less than five seconds is one of my favourite parts of the whole record!'
Charles Layton

'The noise vignette at the end was just something I made at home. I was quite surprised, though pleased, that David chose to use it.'
Graeme Ramsay

'I'm really wearing my influences on my sleeve on this one! I wanted the chorus to sound like 'Wire.' They're one of my favourite groups, but the reference might have been lost on some of the younger members of the band because I first saw them in 1978! We were lucky enough to play with them in Montréal a couple of years ago, though. And then, also, the "How does a girl like you get to be a girl like you?" line comes from one of my other loves, the cinema. Cary Grant's character says it to Eva Marie Saint's in Alfred Hitchcock's brilliant *North By Northwest*. For those who're interested, her reply is: "Lucky, I guess!"'
David Gedge

'When it comes to time signatures in songs I'm pretty much a no nonsense '4/4' man. 4/4 is also called 'common time,' presumably because most pop songs are written in it. It's just your basic rock beat, really. So it was great, of course, having Graeme coming up with guitar parts for Valentina because, since he's also a drummer, some of his ideas were based on less obvious rhythms. This song's a case in point. When he first explained the instrumental section to me I was totally baffled. It just didn't seem to make sense. What made it worse was that the other two seemed to get it straight away. So there was Charlie throwing in these amazing drum-fills and Pepe rocking out with him... and I'd be there, quietly playing along in the hope that no one would notice I didn't have a clue where I was. I felt like the new kid at school. But once I mastered it, of course, it all made perfect sense and now I'm really keen on the irregular nature of it.'
David Gedge

'This is a funny little number... and a tough one to play live. We originally demo-ed it just before David's first 'At The Edge Of The Sea' festival in Brighton in 2009. The demos were actually recorded on the stage at Concorde 2, the venue where 'At The Edge Of The Sea' takes place every year.'
Charles Layton

'I guess this is my equivalent of the "Ruby... don't take your love to town" lyric... the old Kenny Rogers song. The words came pretty quickly but it took me weeks, literally, to hit upon a title I was happy with. So it was a real 'Eureka!' moment when it finally came to me.'
David Gedge

05. STOP THIEF!

YOU'RE IN SO MANY OF HER DREAMS THAT
THERE'S NO ROOM LEFT, IT SEEMS, FOR ME
AND I CURSE THE DAY YOU MET AND I'M
BEGGING YOU TO SET HER FREE

YOU'VE OPENED DOORS FOR HER AND THAT'S
GOOD, IN WAYS I NEVER COULD, I KNOW
BUT NOW YOU'RE CLOSING ONE ON ME AND
THERE'S NOWHERE I CAN SEE TO GO

YOU COULD HAVE ANYONE YOU WANT SO JUST
HAVE SOME DEBUTANTE, NOT HER
OH, CAN'T YOU DISAPPEAR TODAY AND LET US BE
THE WAY WE WERE?

SO IT IS UP TO YOU NOW THEN, PLEASE THINK
ABOUT THIS WHEN YOU CHOOSE
WHEN SOMEONE'S FEELING THIS BEREFT
THERE'S REALLY NOT MUCH LEFT TO LOSE

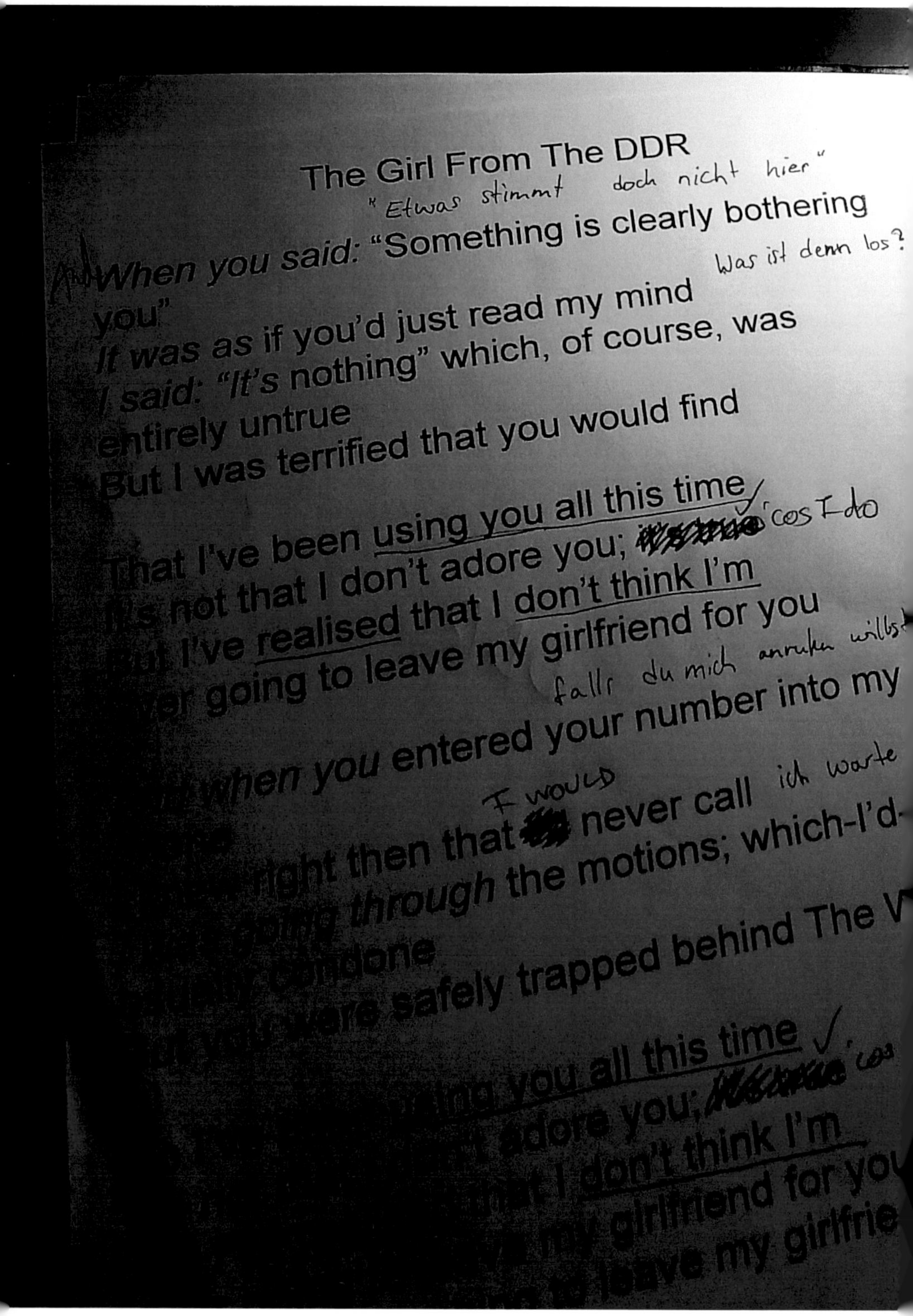

The Girl From The DDR

"Etwas stimmt doch nicht hier"

When you said: "Something is clearly bothering you"

Was ist denn los?

It was as if you'd just read my mind

I said: "It's nothing" which, of course, was entirely untrue

But I was terrified that you would find

That I've been using you all this time

'cos I do

It's not that I don't adore you;

But I've realised that I don't think I'm

...ver going to leave my girlfriend for you

falls du mich anrufen willst

...*when you* entered your number into my

...

I would

...right then that ... never call ich warte

...*going through* the motions; which-I'd-

...condone

...you were safely trapped behind The W...

...using you all this time

...adore you; 'cos

...that I don't think I'm

...my girlfriend for you

...to leave my girlfrie...

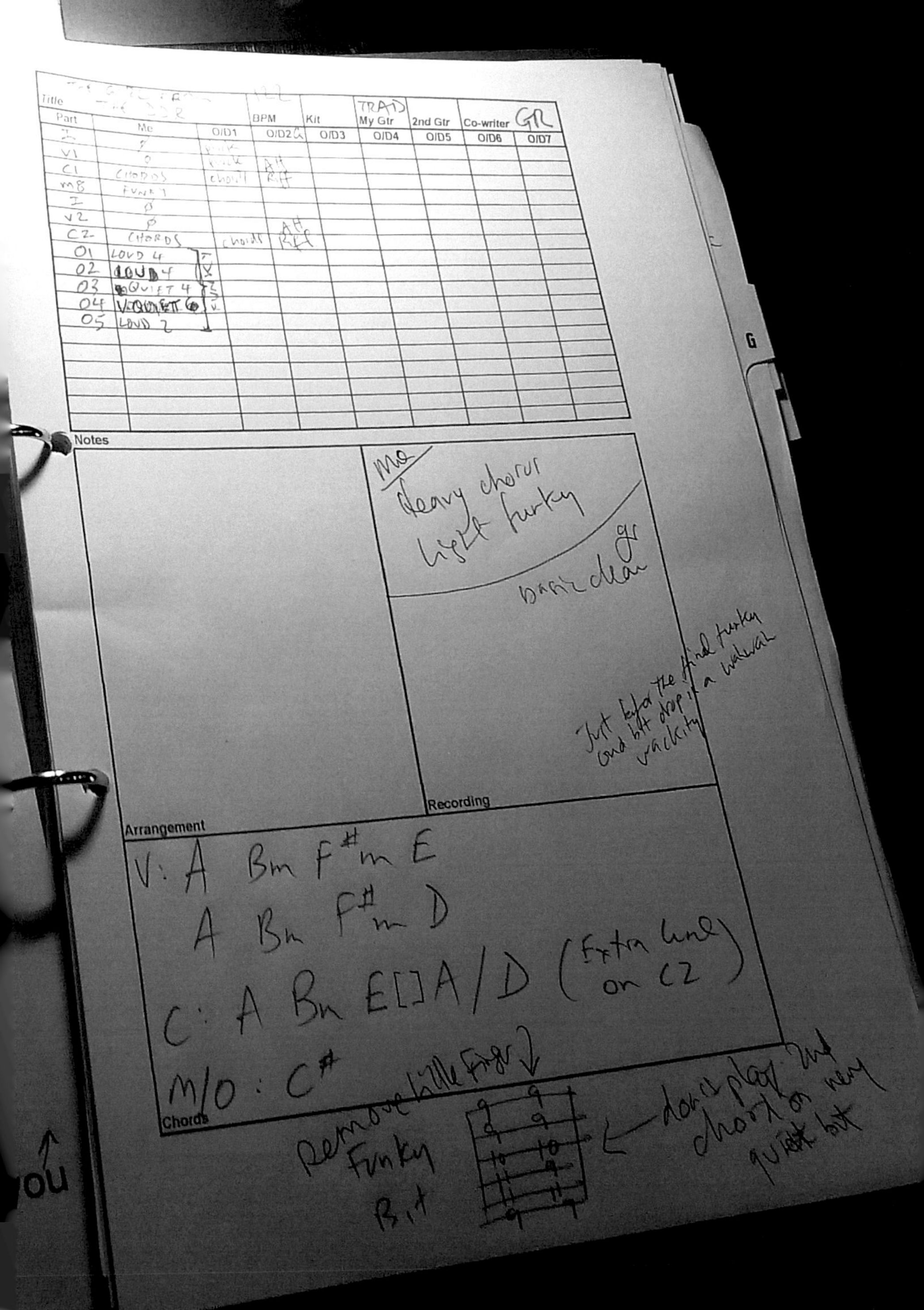

Title
Part
Me
BPM
Kit
TRAD
My Gtr
2nd Gtr
Co-writer
GR
O/D1
O/D2
O/D3
O/D4
O/D5
O/D6
O/D7
CHORDS
FUNKY
CHORDS
LOUD 4
LOUD 4
QUIET 4
LOUD 2
Notes
me
heavy chorus
light funky
basic clean
Recording
Arrangement
V: A Bm F#m E
A Bm F#m D
C: A Bm E[]A/D (Extra line on C2)
M/O: C#
Chords
Remove little finger
Funky Bit
don't play 2nd chord on new quiet bit
G
you

06. THE GIRL FROM THE DDR

HIM:

AND WHEN YOU SAID:
"SOMETHING IS CLEARLY BOTHERING YOU,"
IT WAS AS IF YOU'D JUST READ MY MIND
I SAID: "IT'S NOTHING" WHICH, OF COURSE,
WAS ENTIRELY UNTRUE
BUT I WAS TERRIFIED THAT YOU WOULD FIND...

HER:

ETWAS STIMMT DOCH NICHT
WAS IST DENN LOS?
WIRKLICH? SOLL ICH'S GLAUBEN?

HIM:

THAT I'VE BEEN USING YOU ALL THIS TIME
AND IT'S NOT THAT I DON'T ADORE YOU (BECAUSE I DO)
BUT I'VE REALISED THAT I DON'T THINK I'M EVER GOING TO
LEAVE MY GIRLFRIEND FOR YOU

HIM:

AND WHEN YOU ENTERED YOUR NUMBER INTO MY 'PHONE
I KNEW, RIGHT THEN, THAT I WOULD NEVER CALL
I WAS GOING THROUGH THE MOTIONS, WHICH I'D NEVER
USUALLY CONDONE, BUT YOU WERE SAFELY TRAPPED
BEHIND 'THE WALL'

HER:

MEINE NUMMER. RUF MICH AN
ICH WARTE AUF DICH
IRGENDWANN, SEHN WIR UNS WIEDER

HIM:

SO I'VE BEEN USING YOU ALL THIS TIME
AND IT'S NOT THAT I DON'T ADORE YOU (BECAUSE I DO)
BUT I'VE REALISED THAT I DON'T THINK I'M EVER GOING TO
LEAVE MY GIRLFRIEND FOR YOU
I'M NEVER GOING TO LEAVE MY GIRLFRIEND FOR YOU

'Being a song about the former East Germa – German backing vocals were an obvious choice. At first I had only one or two lines in the verses. But the dual langua singing worked well, so we decided to pu more on it. Now the verses are a dialogu between David and the girl from the DDR. enjoy singing in German because, for onc I don't have to concentrate so hard abou proper English pronunciation!'

Pepe le Moko

'I had to chuckle to myself when Graeme first came in and said here's a new idea have. "What... that joke thing from soun check?!" But it turned out to be a great pop song. I love the 60's 'wig-out' part and the extended quiet bit at the end. Every time we'd play the last five second in rehearsals it felt like the introducti to a game show, so I'd say "Good evening and welcome!"'

Charles Layton

'I've always been interested in the culture of the former Eastern Bloc. In the early days of The Wedding Present we used to travel to West Berlin via 'transit routes' across East Germany and, in 1988, we actually played at the enormous Werner-Seelenbinder-Halle in East Berlin, which was a fascinating experience. So I suppose I've always had some kind of plan to write a song about it. When Swiss national Pepe (who's fluent in German) joined the band in 2010, I took the opportunity to write our first bilingual duet. Charlie's (German) girlfriend, Sarah, pointed out that, since the title is in English, it should really be GDR (German Democratic Republic) rather than DDR (Deutsche Demokratische Republik). She's correct, of course, but I decided to stick with DDR because that's what I've always called it. And it's my song. Ha. People have also speculated whether mobile phones (mentioned in the lyric) were around at that time, too. But I definitely had one in 1988, yes!'
David Gedge

'The opening guitar part was born of what was essentially a gag; a riff I played to amuse Terry on a North American tour, based on the un-subtlety of the distortion pedal (a 'Way Huge Swollen Pickle') that I'd recently spent all my money on. It definitely kept a tongue-in-cheek feel and reminds me of Super Furry Animals a bit. There's an ironic 'quote' from Dalliance in the verses.'
Graeme Ramsay

LE GAS
LA Hte BERGÉE

'This one started as a jaunty (bordering on twee) little riff. It reminded us of 'Holly Jolly Hollywood', in that the chorus sounded... festive. We kept singing, 'Merry-Christmastime...' in the breakdown. Oh, we had a laugh. But it turned into something altogether more aggressive and perhaps this happened in order to counteract the 'Christmas' in it. Or maybe it just happened naturally. It's an aspect of the process I've always enjoyed, how some songs arrive fully formed and others shift around and become something that hardly resembles what they start as.'
Terry de Castro

'This quickly became the best Wedding Present song to play live - without fail, any gig not going well could be redeemed from the monster instrumental section onwards.'
Graeme Ramsay

'When we started playing this live I used to sing the line in the quiet bit as: "If I was a painter, I'd just paint portraits of you," until my friend Dawn Hurst pointed out that the third word should be 'were'. How embarrassing...'
David Gedge

'I remember that we weren't too keen on this song until we arrived in America for the *Bizarro* Tour rehearsals. Then we looked at it again and decided on the verse pattern with the bass and drums. When it locked in, it changed the whole feel of the song. Then, as we began to play it live, it really came together and started going down really well with the crowds. The noisy part at the end was originally a third shorter, but it sounded so good we thought we could extend it so that David and Graeme could kick in with another pedal to go "one louder"!'
Charles Layton

'This is definitely one of my favourites. I wouldn't mind if it was twice as long. I loved it from the first time I heard it in rehearsals; it got me really excited to mix the record.'
Andrew Scheps

'The clattering sound in the quiet end section reprise thing is me, falling over one of those standing ashtray things, as I was trying to film Graeme playing the organ outside in the studio courtyard.'
David Gedge

07. DEER CAUGHT IN THE HEADLIGHTS

YOU WON'T GIVE IT A THOUGHT AND THAT'S NEITHER WRONG NOR RIGHT
BUT I'M THE DEER THAT'S CAUGHT IN YOUR HEADLIGHT
AND HOW CAN IT BE THAT JUST ONE GLANCE IS ENOUGH TO PETRIFY ME?
HOW DO YOU DO THAT STUFF?

BECAUSE AS SOON AS YOU LOOK MY WAY, THAT'S WHEN I TOTALLY FREEZE
AND IT'S AT MOMENTS LIKE THESE THAT I CAN'T THINK OF A SINGLE THING
TO SAY EXCEPT FOR, WELL, MAYBE: "YOU'RE JUST TOO PRETTY FOR ME"

YOU WEAR A STUNNING DRESS AND THEN SAY: "WHAT, THIS OLD THING?!"
AND THE INGENUOUSNESS IS JUST SO CAPTIVATING

AND AS SOON AS YOU LOOK MY WAY, THAT'S WHEN I TOTALLY FREEZE
AND IT'S AT MOMENTS LIKE THESE THAT I CAN'T THINK OF A SINGLE THING
TO SAY EXCEPT FOR, WELL, MAYBE: "YOU'RE JUST TOO PRETTY FOR ME"

AND IF I WERE A PAINTER I'D JUST PAINT PORTRAITS OF YOU
YOU'D BE IN EVERYTHING I DO

08. 524 FIDELIO

IN AMONGST THE STARS: 524 FIDELIO
BETWEEN JUPITER AND MARS
WHEREVER YOU GO, I'LL GO

EFFORTLESSLY CHIC
WITH SCARCELY ANY MAKE-UP
YOU'RE REALLY QUITE UNIQUE FROM THE SECOND THAT YOU WAKE UP

RECKLESS COMMENTS NOTWITHSTANDING, THERE'S ONE THING I MUST DO
RIGHT HERE, RIGHT NOW, HERE'S ME HANDING MY WHOLE LIFE TO YOU
AND THE THINGS I'M SAYING HERE I WON'T REGRET BECAUSE I'D MISS
YOU EVEN IF WE'D NEVER MET

SOMEWHERE IN THE SKY: 524 FIDELIO
DON'T EVER SAY "GOOD-BYE" BECAUSE WHAT I'D DO, I DON'T KNOW

DON'T JOKE ABOUT IT, PLEASE (PRETENDING THAT YOU'RE LEAVING)
I'M DOWN HERE ON MY KNEES
HOW MORE EMBARRASSING COULD THIS BE?

RECKLESS COMMENTS NOTWITHSTANDING, THERE'S ONE THING I MUST
DO RIGHT HERE, RIGHT NOW, HERE'S ME HANDING MY WHOLE LIFE TO YOU
AND THE THINGS I'M SAYING HERE I WON'T REGRET BECAUSE I'D MISS
YOU EVEN IF WE'D NEVER MET

'Graeme came in and said that he had an idea in a 7/8 time signature. I played around with various complicated parts but I was really just making hard work for myself, which is something that you don't want to do, especially when it then comes to playing the track live. Then Graeme told me how he would simplify it himself and that's what I ended up playing. Oh, the joys of having another drummer in the band!'
Charles Layton

''524 Fidelio' was the first song I heard from the album recording sessions. Since I hadn't been involved since the first couple rounds of arrangements and demos, I was intrigued to hear how it had all turned out. My first impression was how very Wedding Present it sounded. I thought the bass was incredibly catchy and the backing vocals sounded rather *Watusi*, but it also had a freshness that sounded new.'
Terry de Castro

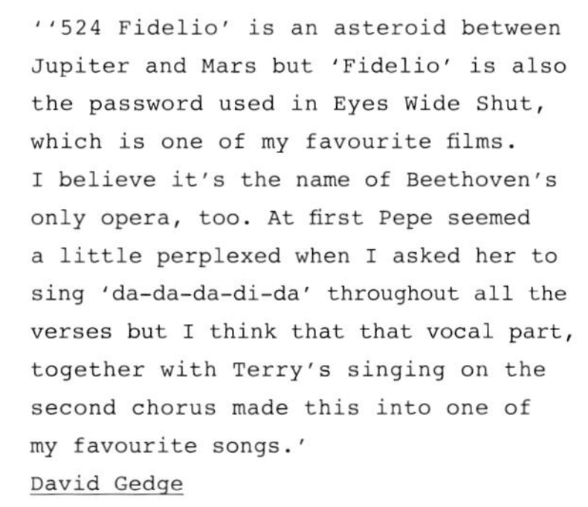

''524 Fidelio' is an asteroid between Jupiter and Mars but 'Fidelio' is also the password used in Eyes Wide Shut, which is one of my favourite films. I believe it's the name of Beethoven's only opera, too. At first Pepe seemed a little perplexed when I asked her to sing 'da-da-da-di-da' throughout all the verses but I think that that vocal part, together with Terry's singing on the second chorus made this into one of my favourite songs.'
David Gedge

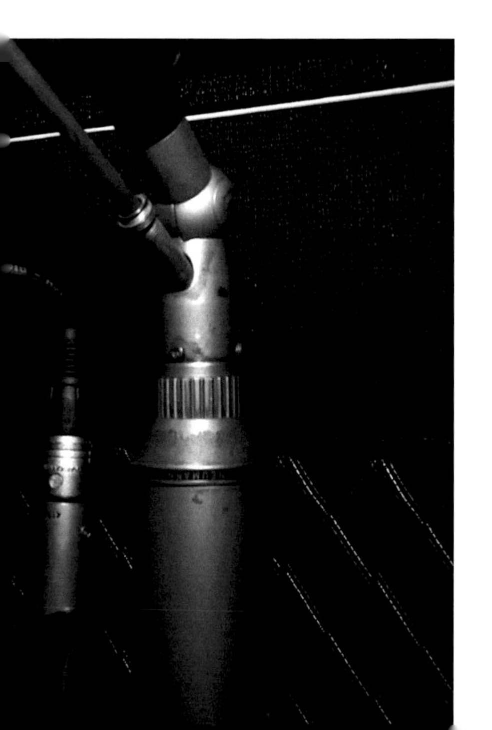

'When we first played it at rehearsal, us rhythm section people had a bit of a bumpy start until we'd thought of parts which did Graeme's guitar riff justice. We got there eventually and what started as a quirky little number turned out to be a very catchy song.'
Pepe le Moko

'The title is like an onion.'
Andrew Scheps

09. END CREDITS

THERE'S NEVER REALLY A GOOD TIME TO SAY GOODBYE
BUT DON'T PRETEND IT'S NOT A RELIEF TO HEAR ME SAY:
"I'M THINKING, RIGHT NOW, MAYBE WE SHOULD END IT"

BECAUSE IT'S TRUE
THE CLOSER I GET TO YOU, THE FURTHER I GET AWAY FROM ME
(THE PERSON THAT I USED TO BE)

IT WASN'T ALWAYS LIKE THIS BEFORE;
THAT WE WERE IN LOVE THERE IS NO DOUBT
BUT I'M NOT HAPPY ANYMORE AND, FOR THAT REASON, I'M OUT

AND IT'S TRUE
THE CLOSER I GET TO YOU, THE FURTHER I GET AWAY FROM ME
(THE PERSON THAT I OUGHT TO BE)

THIS IS NO LONGER ANY FUN
THIS COUPLE WILL NEVER BE STROLLING
INTO A BLOOD RED SETTING SUN WHILE THE END CREDITS ARE ROLLING

YES, IT'S TRUE
THE CLOSER I GET TO YOU, THE FURTHER I GET AWAY FROM ME
(THE PERSON THAT I WANT TO BE)

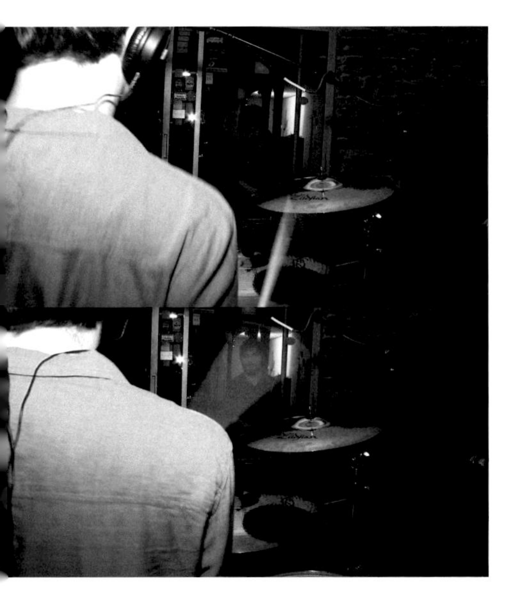

'Two drummers in one band? HELLO! For live purposes, this had to be a song that David could play alone on the guitar, of course, but he's helped by Pepe because the bass is a real driving force. In terms of the drums, Graeme just plays bass drum, snare and high hats. I wanted him to play a full kit, but he isn't a 'show off' kind of guy. But we have different drum styles and he can get far more out of three things than I can, anyway. I love the fact that there's a bass solo, too!'
Charles Layton

'This is a bass player's dream come true; two drummers and a loud soaring bass line with a little crazy solo bit. My Boss overdrive pedal was perfect for this track, it gives it a big fat driven sound with a lot of presence. My guilty pleasure!'
Pepe le Moko

'Rather than to show off that I could drum as well as hack the guitar, this was intended to make a feature of David's 'other' signature guitar sound – a Stratocaster with four strings tuned to E - which I thought had been missing from 'post-Cinerama' Wedding Present. For my money this one came out most favourably of all the songs we recorded.'
Graeme Ramsay

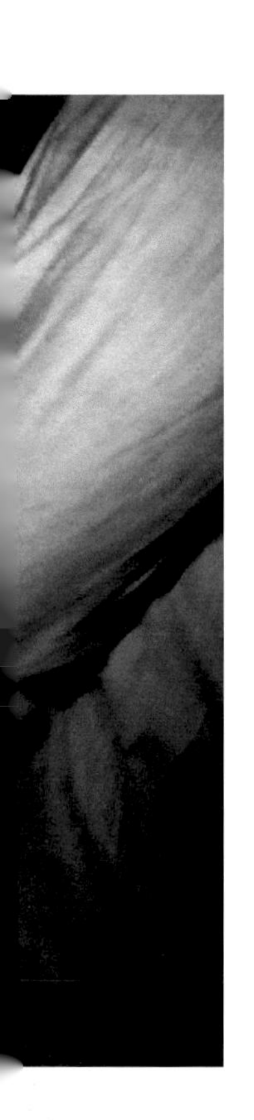

'When we did the first demo of it, Charlie and Graeme set up the two drum kits, and off they went. It sounded so cool! You could see how much they were both enjoying it and we recorded the first take on an 8-track recorder. It was pretty spontaneous and the take was near perfect, so we left it at that. At the end of the day I went to unplug an amp or something but accidentally unplugged the machine we'd recorded it on. And the songs hadn't been saved. There was a horrible moment of panic, until we realised that it was on a different digital 'reel' and I had only erased songs we'd already saved and not the one-and-only original two-drummer take. If that had happened, I doubt Charlie would be still be speaking to me, even years later!'
Terry de Castro

'I love that this mix is actually two mono mixes, each with its own drum kit and guitar. Just listen to one speaker at a time and see!'
Andrew Scheps

'Graeme told me that the idea for this song came to him in the shower, with the bass and guitar riffs playing off each other. A few months later we're sitting on the sofa in David's living room working on the bass and guitar. It's so mundane it's interesting, if that makes sense? It reminds me how David sometimes talks about how weird it is that just because he wrote a bunch of songs in his bedroom, a mere few months later he's loading tour t-shirts into a van.'
Terry de Castro

'Instrumentally this was the one I was most attached to at the writing stage. However, I'll always associate it with the unbearable clanger I made playing it in London in 2010 on the *Bizarro* tour.'
Graeme Ramsay

'Another song that went through different stages of arrangement. When we played it live during the *Bizarro* tour, the entire quiet introductory section was repeated in the middle of the song. I don't know whether it is the straight-to-the-point Swiss nature of mine or just personal preference, but I felt that this section went on for too long. So when we had the final rehearsals before recording, I managed to convince the others to shorten it.'
Pepe le Moko

'This song really grew on me. At first I really didn't think anything of it. Originally the chorus wasn't repeated at the end and Graeme wasn't convinced by the idea of reprising it when we discussed it during rehearsals. But it's too good to only have it appearing just once. The voice-over by the lovely Sayaka Amano is great as well. David wrote what he wanted her to translate... but I like to think that she's talking about ice cream or something equally banal.'
Charles Layton

'The Japanese narration on the end is there to suggest the feeling of alienatic that comes from being a long way from home. For the jet-lagged travelling Englishman, Japan can often seem completely bizarre. I think this is a beautiful way to finish the album, if I say so myself! The only sad thing for me is that Graeme left the band shortly aft we'd finished recording and so he wasn't there when we played this live in Japan, one of his favourite places... and were joined by Sayaka onstage.'
David Gedge

10. MYSTERY DATE

HIM:

I CAN'T STAND THIS APPREHENSION
MAYBE WE SHOULD KISS TO BREAK THE TENSION?
AND I KEEP TELLING MYSELF: "YES, IT'S TRUE,
I REALLY AM JUST SITTING HERE ALONE WITH YOU"

AND NO ONE COULD'VE BEEN MORE SURPRISED THAN ME
WHEN YOU WROTE YOUR NUMBER DOWN AND SAID:
"CALL ME AT THE FIRST OPPORTUNITY"

BECAUSE THIS DOES NOT HAPPEN TO ME
THINGS LIKE THIS DO NOT HAPPEN TO ME
THIS DOES NOT HAPPEN TO ME
THINGS LIKE THIS DO NOT HAPPEN TO ME

THIS DOES NOT HAPPEN TO ME
THINGS LIKE THIS DO NOT HAPPEN TO ME
THIS DOES NOT HAPPEN TO ME
THINGS LIKE THIS DO NOT HAPPEN TO ME

HER:

MAINICHI KONO KOUENNI ANATAGA SUWAATEIRUNOWO
SHIITERUYO KOKOWA IGIRISUSHIKINOTEIEN
ANATAWA IGIRISKARA KITANO?
HOME SHIIKUNI NAATERUNO?
SOUIUFUUNI MIERUKEDO DAIJYOUBU?
NIHONNI TOMODACHIWA IRU?
MOSHI YOKAATARA TOMODACHINI NAATE KUREMASENKA?
HAI, KORE WATASHINO BANGOU
ITUDEMO RENRAKUSHITE!
SOSHITARA DE-TOSHIMASYO!

LOS ANGELES

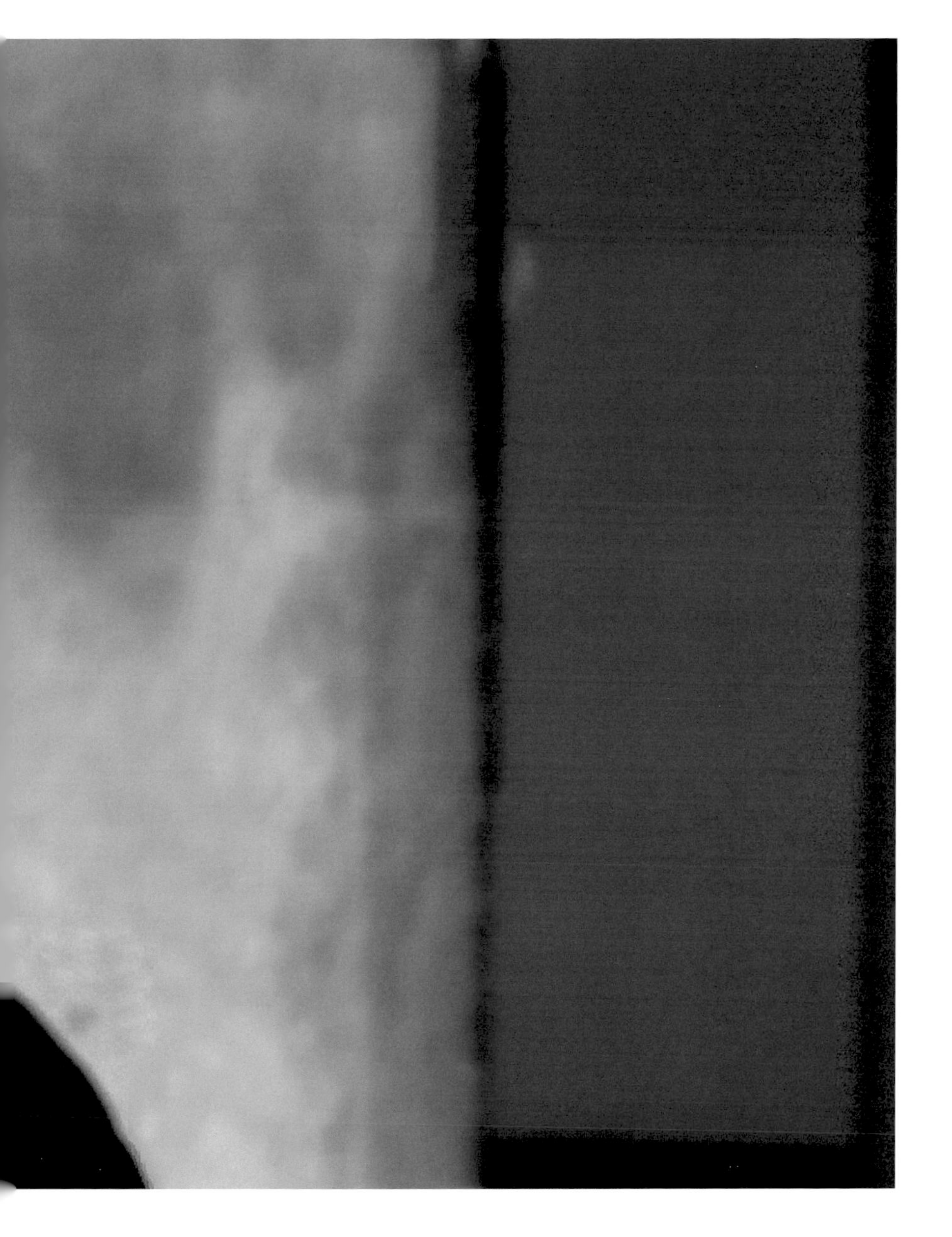

'This opening riff is Jet Age-influenced, I reckon. They were our touring partners in 2010. I want to say it's Who-y but I was never an avid Who listener. Charlie plays toms in a cool, enthusiastic and triumphant-sounding way and I remember thinking that what he did on this one was great.'

Graeme Ramsay

'Pepe kills it on this one!'

Andrew Scheps

'David wasn't totally happy about his vocals and so he gave me the task of transforming the song into a masterpiece... using the backing vocals! His idea was for me to sing the entire verse vocals, along with him, in unison. And so I did. It was quite tricky to get my vocals completely in sync with David's singing – I had to turn on my inner Gedge brain and memorise his entire phrasing. And, after all the effort I put into getting it right, it wasn't even used in the final mix! Ah well, such is life. The chorus still has backing vocals though, so it wasn't all for nothing...'

Pepe le Moko

'I love playing the toms and this song just called out for it. The verse reminds me of 'Click, Click''

Charles Layton

''Journey Into Space' was a science fiction drama written for BBC radio in the 1950s and the 'Don't you want to go to the place where the rainbow ends?' line is another steal from *Eyes Wide Shut*. I like this song, but after such a 'statement' musical introduction, I personally feel that it's let down by my vocal melody in the verse. I was going to totally re-write it, actually, but Graeme talked me out of it, saying that he liked it. I love the singing that Pepe does in the chorus, though. She transforms the part in the same way that she did with 'You Jane''

David Gedge

01. JOURNEY INTO SPACE

I KNOW I SHOULDN'T BUT I CAN'T STOP MYSELF COMING HERE
AND YOU DON'T EXACTLY TRY TO DISSUADE ME, SO I'LL PERSEVERE
DON'T YOU WANT TO GO TO THE PLACE WHERE THE RAINBOW ENDS?
WELL, YOU'RE THE WOMAN WHO ONCE SAID:
"WE'RE MORE THAN JUST FRIENDS"

YOU KNOW AS WELL I DO, HE'S JUST NOT GOOD ENOUGH FOR YOU
SO I'VE DECIDED THAT IT WAS TIME I CAME TO YOUR RESCUE
THIS IS NOT THE MOMENT FOR OVER ANALYSIS
THERE'S NO CHANCE HE'LL EVER FIND OUT ABOUT ANY OF THIS

HALF OF YOU SAYS: "I SHOULDN'T," HALF OF YOU SAYS: "I SHOULD"
HALF OF YOU SAYS: "I WOULDN'T," HALF OF YOU SAYS: "I WOULD"

YOU NEED TO GET OUT OF THIS PLACE
AND TAKE A JOURNEY INTO SPACE

HALF OF YOU SAYS: "I SHOULDN'T," HALF OF YOU SAYS: "I SHOULD"
HALF OF YOU SAYS: "I WOULDN'T," HALF OF YOU SAYS: "I WOULD"

BUT, YOU KNOW, I SHAKE WITH LONGING WHENEVER I HOLD YOU
OH, WON'T YOU STAY WITH ME? (WE'LL HAVE THE NIGHT OF OUR LIVES!)
YOU DON'T HAVE WORRY, I'VE ALREADY TOLD YOU
YOU DON'T HAVE TO RUN AWAY WITH ME
NO ONE MENTIONED HUSBANDS AND WIVES

02. 1000 FAHRENHEIT

WITH THOSE TANTALISING EYES
ALL THE GIRLS WANT TO BE HER
AND THE POWER TO TERRORISE
ALL THE GIRLS WANT TO BE HER
AND ALL THE BOYS WANT TO BE WITH HER

I WISH I COULD WALK AWAY
YOU MIGHT BUT I DON'T HAVE THE POWER TO DISOBEY
YOU DO BUT I DON'T
AND YOU'RE RIGHT, NO I WON'T

SHE SAID: "IT'S GETTING WARMER, IT'S GETTING WARMER,
IT'S GETTING WARMER, IT'S LIKE A THOUSAND FAHRENHEIT"
SHE SAID: "DON'T YOU WANT TO, DON'T YOU WANT TO,
DON'T YOU WANT TO BE MY BOYFRIEND TONIGHT?"

WHEN SHE GIVES THAT KNOWING LOOK YOU KNOW
IT'S NOT GOING TO TURN OUT WELL
BECAUSE YOU'RE DANGLING ON A HOOK
EVEN THOUGH YOU COULDN'T TELL BECAUSE YOU'RE
COMPLETELY UNDER HER SPELL

SHE SAID: "IT'S GETTING WARMER, IT'S GETTING WARMER,
IT'S GETTING WARMER, IT'S LIKE A THOUSAND FAHRENHEIT"
SHE SAID: "DON'T YOU WANT TO, DON'T YOU WANT TO,
DON'T YOU WANT TO BE MY BOYFRIEND TONIGHT?"

SHE SAID: "I'LL CALL YOU WHEN I CAN"
BUT WHEN SHE NOTICED MY DESPONDENCY
SHE SAID: "I REALLY LIKE A MAN WHO KNOWS WHERE HE
WANTS TO BE, ESPECIALLY IF IT'S HERE WITH ME"

SHE SAID: "IT'S GETTING WARMER, IT'S GETTING WARMER,
IT'S GETTING WARMER, IT'S LIKE A THOUSAND FAHRENHEIT"
SHE SAID: "DON'T YOU WANT TO, DON'T YOU WANT TO,
DON'T YOU WANT TO BE MY BOYFRIEND TONIGHT?"

SHE SAID: "IT'S GETTING WARMER, IT'S GETTING WARMER,
IT'S GETTING WARMER, IT'S LIKE A THOUSAND FAHRENHEIT"
SHE SAID: "DON'T YOU WANT TO, DON'T YOU WANT TO,
DON'T YOU WANT TO BE MY BOYFRIEND TONIGHT?"

'Now we're rockin'!'
David Gedge

'This was one of the last songs written. Another upbeat number... I think we just decided that it should be played as fast possible... which is about 206BPM! I love a snare roll and it seemed to fit well over the chorus, so we stuck with it.'
Charles Layton

'This one boasts one of my favourite split-seconds out of everything that we recorded. The piano sustain during the breakdown makes this dreamy chord - I haven't really thought about what it is - and it creates such a contrast, not just to the rest of the song as intended but to the whole lot. I think it takes you miles away into something very different - but suddenly it's gone and you're back in the urgency and immediacy of the verse. I should point out that it was an accident and not some stroke of genius I could claim!'
Graeme Ramsay

'I love this song, but the really short instrumental is my favorite part. It reminds me of Eno's ambient albums (and that's a good thing!)'
Andrew Scheps

'I can hardly believe that this song didn't make it onto the final album track listing, but I guess we had to draw a line somewhere.'
Pepe le Moko

'Andrew Sheps came to the final rehearsal before we started recording. On listening to 'Pain Perdu', he suggested we make the end even heavier. We took his advice to heart and when we were at Black Box, I tried out a couple of ideas on the bass. David suggested that I down-tune the E string and that very effectively did the job. That part suddenly had a heavy metal feel to it, just by playing it harder and including that lower D. I really enjoyed recording it and probably had a big grin on my face. I felt like Lemmy!'
Pepe le Moko

03. PAIN PERDU

I WONDER IF YOU STILL SEE PEOPLE THAT WE USED TO KNOW
I WONDER IF YOU STILL GO TO PLACES THAT WE USED TO GO
I WONDER IF YOU STILL LISTEN TO THE BANDS WE USED TO SEE
I WONDER IF YOU STILL WATCH THE SAME TV SHOWS AS ME

I'D LIKE TO KNOW [DON'T ASK ME WHY I DO]
IT'S A LIFETIME AGO BUT I CAN'T FORGET YOU

I WONDER IF YOU STILL LIE WHEN SOMEBODY ASKS YOUR AGE
I WONDER IF YOU STILL SPOIL STORIES BY READING
THE LAST PAGE

I'D LIKE TO KNOW [DON'T ASK ME WHY I DO]
IT'S A LIFETIME AGO BUT I CAN'T FORGET YOU

AND IN ALL OF THE YEARS SINCE THEN AND,
THIS IS SUCH A DUMB THING
I JUST CAN'T HELP IT, I THINK ABOUT YOU EVERY DAY
AND IN ALL OF THE YEARS WHEN
I THOUGHT I WAS LOOKING FOR SOMETHING
I ALREADY HAD IT AND THEN I THREW IT AWAY

I WONDER IF YOU STILL CRY WHEN YOU READ
SOME SOPPY BOOK
I WONDER IF YOU STILL LAUGH WHEN
YOUR GRANDMOTHER SAYS: "FUCK"

I'D LIKE TO KNOW [DON'T ASK ME WHY I DO]
IT'S A LIFETIME AGO BUT I CAN'T FORGET YOU

AND IN ALL OF THE YEARS SINCE THEN AND,
THIS IS SUCH A DUMB THING
I JUST CAN'T HELP IT, I THINK ABOUT YOU EVERY DAY
AND IN ALL OF THE YEARS WHEN
I THOUGHT I WAS LOOKING FOR SOMETHING
I ALREADY HAD IT AND THEN I THREW IT AWAY

''Pain Perdu' is what French people call the dish that Americans refer to as 'French Toast'... and which we British call 'Eggy Bread'. Too much information? OK... how about this? After we'd decided that it wasn't heading for the album we decided to let iTunes have this track as an extra download thing. One of my lines in the song uses the word 'fuck,' though, and since iTunes have rules about swearing we decided to do a mix – 'Pain Perdu [Censored Version]' – which had that word muted. Guess which version I mistakenly sent to iTunes? People on Twitter were saying... "If that's the censored version I'd hate to hear the uncensored one!"'
David Gedge

'I wondered if this one maybe went a bit too far with the 'quirky' thing - possibly too many 'feel' changes. After we played this live some fans commented to me that the (then) new songs were sounding 'complicated' due to all the time changes and I was a bit concerned that we were doing the wrong thing. None of it is contrived in the slightest, I think my train of thought in writing is just prone to jumps and hops like that.'
Graeme Ramsay

'This was my favourite song when we started working on it. I thought it was such a quirky Graeme riff and I loved playing it. And then when David put the lyrics to it I liked it even more. They're classic, clever Gedge lyrics. When we came up with the fast stop-start bit, there was a knock on the door of the rehearsal room and David said 'Ha... I bet that's the 'Stupid Tempo Change Police'!'
Terry de Castro

04. CAN YOU KEEP A SECRET?

YOU JUST OVERHEARD A WHISPERED WORD;
DO YOU REALLY STILL WANT TO GO THERE?
YOU ASK WHAT'S GOING ON
WELL, YES, THERE IS SOMEONE
(IN FACT YOU ALREADY KNOW HER)

AND, YES, THE FLIRTING WENT TOO FAR
NOW THERE'S NO GOING BACK

AND I CAN'T WALK AWAY; I HAVE TO STAY
(THIS IS BIGGER THAN YOU THINK)
SHE'S NOT THE KIND OF GIRL YOU FIND WHEN YOU'VE
JUST HAD TOO MUCH TO DRINK

SO, YES, THE FLIRTING WENT TOO FAR
NOW THERE'S NO GOING BACK

AND THAT'S HOW I ENDED UP IN THIS AFFAIR BUT,
YOU KNOW, I DON'T CARE
BUT THAT'S WHY I'M MAKING UP ALIBIS THAT I HOPE
DON'T SOUND LIKE LIES

THAT'S HOW I ENDED UP IN THIS AFFAIR BUT,
YOU KNOW, I DON'T CARE
BUT THAT'S WHY I'M MAKING UP ALIBIS THAT I HOPE
DON'T SOUND LIKE LIES

AND NOW YOU KNOW I HAVE TO ASK YOU
IF YOU CAN KEEP A SECRET
NOW YOU KNOW I HAVE TO ASK YOU
IF YOU CAN KEEP A SECRET
HEY!

'One of the first songs that was written. Boring drum fact... it's the only song played with the brushes. As we had a fair few tracks at the time that had long outros, it was decided that this would rise and fall at the end. I love the way it flows.'
Charles Layton

'This is one of my favourite Wedding Present songs to play live. It is such a big journey of emotions, sounds and energy and it always feels very epic when playing it. It starts so calmly before slowly evolving into something bigger – it's like the music takes you into a state of trance. I think we managed to capture the changes and developments within the song really well in the recording.'
Pepe le Moko

'When I heard the rough mix of this song I was surprised (in a good way) at how long the outro became. I liked the hypnotic quality of it. And I also absolutely love David's little arpeggio on the middle eight, too. He said it was just a bog-standard riff, but this just goes to show you how things can really transform and work brilliantl in different contexts.'
Terry de Castro

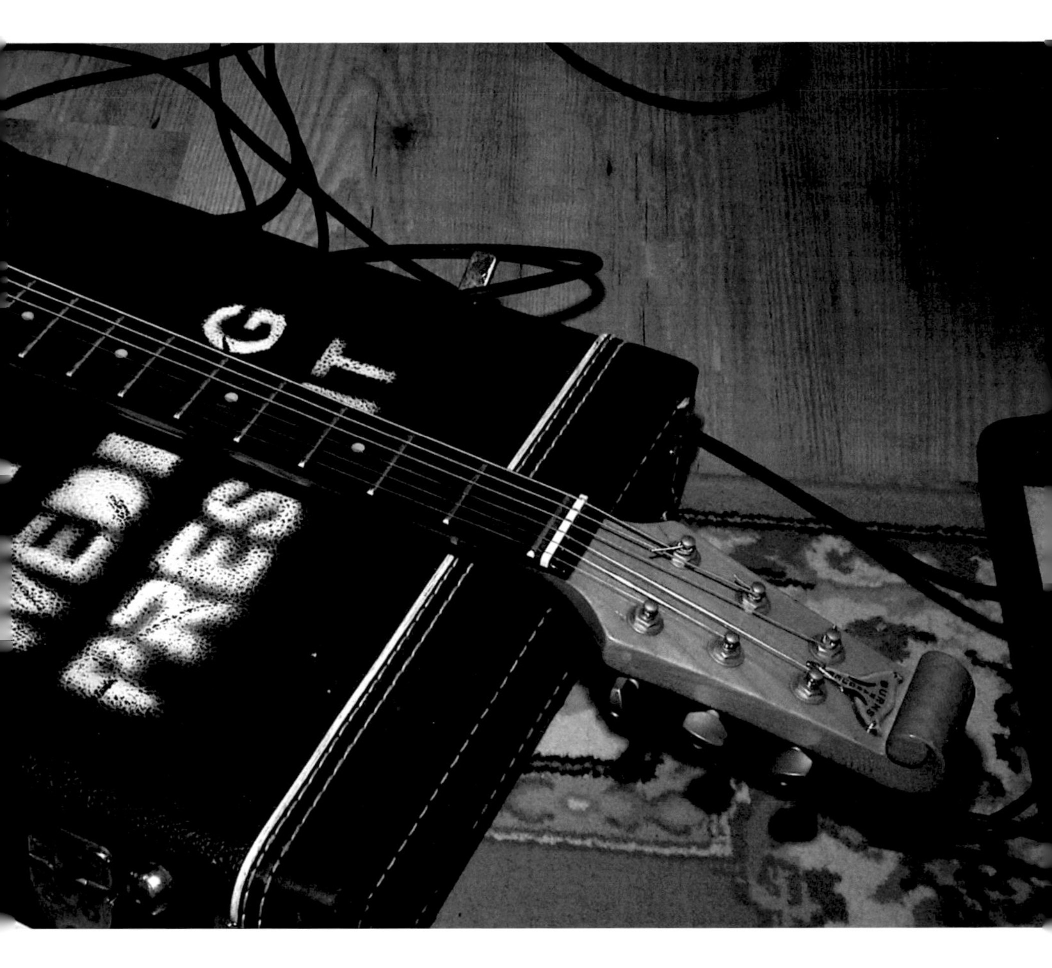

see this one as very
erry' - not least because
e backing vocal is
cellent. I think the feel
the song was pretty well
tablished from the time she
ought the riff to the group,
o. I felt a little bit self-
nscious about the middle
ght section because it's a
e bit 'rock', harmonically;
also wasn't too sure I had
e guitar technique for the
ort of) lead part – it's got
nd of a Jane's Addiction
und to my ears.'
aeme Ramsay

'Graeme's playing on this track
is outstanding... which is
odd for someone who doesn't
think they're very good on
the guitar! I don't want to
sound like I'm blowing our own
trumpet, but there are more
good musical ideas in this one
song that a lot bands have on
an entire album!'
David Gedge

ORANGE

VOX
REX
SOVTEK
SOUND CITY
Stark
VOX

All songs written & published by David Gedge & Graeme Ramsay except 'Deer Caught In The Headlights' and 'Can You Keep A Secret?' (written & published by David Gedge & Terry de Castro). All publishing administered by Fintage Music International outside of The United Kingdom and Eire.

All songs arranged by David Gedge, Graeme Ramsay, Charles Layton, Pepe le Moko & Terry de Castro at Brighton Electric (Brighton, England) with assistance from Andrew Scheps.

Performed by The Wedding Present.

David Gedge
Singing, Guitars & Percussion.
Graeme Ramsay
Guitars, Piano, Harmonium & Second Drum Kit on 'End Credits'.
Pepe le Moko
Bass & Backing Vocals.
Charles Layton
Drums & Percussion.

Additional backing vocals by Terry de Castro.
Japanese narration on 'Mystery Date' by Sayaka Amano.
The two drum kits recorded on 'End Credits' are panned in the mix, with Charles Layton in the left channel and Graeme Ramsay in the right channel.

Produced By Andrew Scheps, David Gedge, Graeme Ramsay, Pepe le Moko, Charles Layton, Peter Deimel, David Odlum & Ulysses Noriega.

Recorded & mixed during the Summer & Autumn of 2011.

Group recorded by Peter Deimel & David Odlum at Black Box Studio (Noyant La Gravoyere, France). David Gedge & Terry De Castro's vocals recorded by Ulysses Noriega at The Laundry Room (Los Angeles, California). Pepe le Moko's vocals recorded by Samuel Beer-Pearce at Allan's Cove (Brighton, England). Mixed by Andrew Scheps at Punkerpad West (Van Nuys, California). Track order sequenced by Graeme Ramsay. Mastered by Andy Pearce and Matt Wortham at Wired Masters (London, England). Translation into German by Pepe le Moko. Translation into Japanese by Shihoko Takahashi.

Album sleeve design by Egelnick & Webb. Album Photography by Jessica McMillan.